Love in Black and White

Urban Poetry

By Amanda Sohan

At Home With A Teacup

The Teacup Ladies

Love In Black And White
Urban Poetry

Text Copyright © 2015 Amanda Sohan
Printed and Published by Amanda Sohan
ISBN 978-0-692-50966-1
www.athomewithateacup.com

To Love & Lovers

Everyone wants something beautiful in
their life. Have no doubt; you are a
thing of beauty - AS

Table of Contents

<u>CCS</u>

You love me through my most unlovable moments and lead me back to the beginning when I lose my way with patience and loving kindness

Your beauty lies in your quiet forbearance.

You are what Pandora left in the box when all the world was burning.

You my love are my hope.

I Am Legend

I have run with the highlanders
through the green Scottish hills

Whispered with the small folk
and chased other Irish thrills

Charmed the cobra with my Indian
ancestors and tasted spice and salt

Danced with Eskimos as the
Northern lights sprang forth

Stormed the plains of Africa with my
brother wildebeest

Padded through the Brazilian jungle
with my sister Tiger in search of feast

The world in words, picture, rhythm and song
The world of vast wonder where everywhere I belong

Through The Ashes

Today they laughed and called me names
Made me eat my guilt and shame
Pelted me with stones and rock
My pain and blood, something to mock

Today they have my neck underfoot
Today they stilled me with a look
Today they hurt me with their words
Today they came in herds and herds

Tomorrow my body will be bruised
Tomorrow I will feel ill and used
Tomorrow I won't have strength of mind
Tomorrow sorrow and tears is all I will find

But someday he assures me this too shall pass
He holds my heart in his hands and promises this will
not last
He wipes my tears and forgives my past
He holds me steady sure and fast

And though today I am in despair
I know he is always and ever near
I am certain that after the rain
HE will lift me up again.

Emissary

You are the candy in my cane
the sugar rush that has no name
the clothes I wear the air I breathe
the perfume in spaces you like to feed
the very soap that washes me clean
the very drug that makes me a fiend

You're every thought in my head
You are the scent in my bed
And when you're gone I turn to stone
Though you go forth I am alone
Cold to the touch and bitter to the taste
Until you return my love. Make haste.

Tweaker

I dream in drams and grams for you
I play in powders of snow
I pinch my nostrils and tap my vein
You keep me in exceeding pain
Make me chase the high that begins with your name
But unlike the first rush it's never the same
I shake and shudder, I cough and shiver
I crave your warmth like an Ocean calls home to the
River
Clean and sober bait me
Coffee mates me
Cigarettes waste me
But I still taste thee
I sleep in fits
Minutes fly, an hour ticks
Groups share
Souls bare
I stare
At long last I sign
On the dotted line
I'm out. I'm free
Lucky me!
An hour later, a nervous twitch
A familiar itch
Where's my stronghold?
Save me before I fold
My hands are shaking as I dial the phone
I sigh in relief, my sponsor is home

Tip the Scales

Life beckons her arms with love
Caresses my face with the warm sunshine above
She uncurls her flowery vine toward me
And invites me to breathe in her wondrous bounty

Her sister death entreats me with sweet surrender
Laden's my eyelids with a butterfly's kiss
Ensures me there will be nothing I miss
And invokes me with her fiery bliss

As I shrug and shift my shoulder
Bouncing the weight of devil and angel
The balancing act formulating one winner
A decision was made for one weary sinner

A Picture Is Worth A Thousand Words

There he sat on his gilded throne
sword in hand, all alone
eyes glistening with unshed tears
unleashed, unearthed were all his fears
a bitter taste left in his mouth
a horrendous death toll led further south
overwhelming sorrow, loss, blood and bone
the sorceress betrayer, a human clone

She warmed his hearth and then his heart
and in one fell swoop ripped both apart
too long too long she sealed his eyes
caresses and kisses, cloaked in a lover's guise

In his hands, the lover she played
in his bed, the enchantress laid
in his head, the web she did spin
and all the while, he was part of her sin

Now come what may, no matter the cost
the king has regained what he once lost
his eyes are open, his heart burns
with rage and horror from all he learns
and with a mighty swing of hand
he cut away at all she planned
with heavy foot he plots and trods
and made it back, his heart at odds
his kingdom half in ruin, in ash and soot
but alas, alas, she is underfoot

He handles the blade and draws her near
cradles her head and wipes her tear
kisses her tender, all so dear
plunges the dirk with delicate fear

She doesn't scream, in truth she smiles
and held his heart with her eyes
the game is lost, the king has won
she fades, she fades and all is done.

Remnants

I'm so glad to see
How well you get along without me
Your face looks bright and aglow
No bags under your eyes, no dark shadow
No painful tenor in your voice
No indecision about your choice
Your new life a picture perfect reflection
No sign or notions of my rejection
She warms your bed and carries your scent in her hair
And made you forget all that we shared
I'm happy for you and the peace you must feel
I suppose you now have something substantial and
real
I ask only one thing if you could find the time
Now that you're so busy and no longer mine
Can you demonstrate how you managed to forget?
Banished our memories with so little regret?
Expelled me from your system in so short a time
When I held your heart as you undoubtedly held mine
Perhaps it's much simpler than I may imagine
And only I felt the love and the passion
I suppose in the end despite all of the tears and
chatter
You're right of course, does it really matter?

Sublime

I tilted the earth
And let the waves crash over me
Driving me under
With roaring thunder
Only darkness around
As I surrender
And let it be
The drowning of both you and me
And the earth righted herself
The waves receding
To join the sea
Carrying the memories
Of both you and me
To a far off place
Across an ocean of time
And I knew once more
You would always and never be mine

Crime Scene

Love me so rough
You leave fingerprints on my skin
If CSI shined a black light
They'd know this body was made for sin
Bite your shoulder, rake my nails across your back
Check under my nails and find traces of your skin
intact

A little blood spatter
Simply doesn't matter
Carpet fibers, DNA
Transferred in the dark of night or light of day

Loving you is criminal
Maximum time seems minimal
Your fingers tighten around my neck
Producing just the right effect
The sheen of sweat, the glazed over eyes
The half open lips in sweet surprise
The dangling cuffs, the ankle ties
The evidential proof measured in soft sighs
La petite mort on the rise

Impasse

I am your slave
Let's misbehave
There's no limit
To how we could do it
Give it a try
Do or die
Inhale me
Turn the key
Unlock my secrets
Exhale your regrets
Let me consume you
Emergency code blue
Give in, let go
Say yes instead of no
I promise you'll enjoy the show
Come on baby, I'm a pro.

Adieu

Can you feel it?
My shadows of love retreating
Leaving you uncovered
Naked, vulnerable
No longer impervious
Flecks of pain
Penetrate
Obliterate
Bet you're attempting to recalculate
You realize my value
But homiE like your past due bills it's way too late
Just like the seeds you artificially inseminate
You bullshit's real
Your game is fake
Oh now you can relate?
All the hoops you made me jump
And like a champ I took my lumps
But it's a new dawn a new day
In the immortal words of Trump
You're fired
Retired
Kick rocks and hit the bricks
Silly rabbit with your silly tricks
It's hunting season
Best believin'
I'm a rabbit slayer
You haven't got a prayer
Kiss kiss, bang bang
It's a done deal
You're no longer my main course
You ain't even a happy meal
How many ways can I say it's over?
Stop tryin' to sway me
It's time to rock a bye you baby

Dis is a worldwide ting
All dem rich gyal a sing
Nuff good man me done pass
But you, I go dus' off
Look at your face, in so much pain
A lifetime will pass but you will remember my name.

<u>By Design</u>

I drew him up in specs and schemes
The making of the man in dreams
Other drafts that came before
Oh contraire and such a bore
A dash of handsome
A spoonful of charm
A pinch of wit
A cup of napalm
An explosion and he entered my life
And caused me heartache, pain and strife
Back to the drawing board I wanted to go
But instead fell to my knees and let go
I told it all, he listened with patience
Even as I questioned why did you make us?
Be still my child
You cannot create
With your thoughts and your hands
That perfect mate
I've been molding one just for you
And if you simply wait you'll be happy too
Soon after, while I was doing my thang
You came along and I let you in
Though it's not always a rose garden, or a picnic or cake
You are definitely my perfect mate.

Castles in the Air

Yesterday you were here
In your bed telling me stories
Sharing your life
Letting me hold you
I was happy and thinking of the tomorrows we would
share

Today I am not there
My heart heavy with worries
Cut off from you
And I am unhappy and thinking of my tomorrows
with fear

Tomorrow you won't be here
I will face the fact
You're not coming back
I want to be hopeful in my thinking
And no longer shower my tomorrows with tears

Beautiful Extremity

I love my toes
If I had my way
There'd be rows and rows
I clip, I snip
Only heaven knows
The time I spend perfecting my beautiful toes

I venture out daily only to show
The world how much I am aglow
Is this rational you ask?
How am I to know?
I'm just in love with my beautiful toes

Journey

The utterance of my name from your lips sets my feet
to path
From whispers on wind, I come
Wait for me
The love I bear knows no barrier
Not even death can keep us apart

Folly

Another day.
I got through another day without hearing from you
Without reaching for you.
I'm sure I should have felt some measure of success,
something won, nothing less.
The opposite occurred - your vice grip even tighter.
Instead of the distance between us making my desire
for you weaken, alas, it has been indeed strengthened
Intensified and fed by daydreams and desire
I am on fire.

How can one feed off of nothing you ask for that is
precisely what you give?
I'll tell you - for I am the source of my own demise.

I talk to you, though you are not here
I think for you and draw you near
I see you through my eyes
Telling myself foul lies

It is I who feed the flame
Touch my lips, whisper your name

Your existence my dream where we two may dwell
forever
My heart and yours, joined by holy tether

It matters not what you think of me.
Leave me my dreams.
My world contained in unstable seams.

Unanswered

All of the letters in my head
All of the things I never said
Locked away deep inside
In the dark, that I must hide
Do you think of me
Or miss my touch?
Did I make you feel far too much?
Questionable, at best
False words I tell myself
To soothe my wounded, weary heart
And pretend that's why you kept us apart.
I'm afraid of the truth, truth be told
Of the choice you made, of the stand you hold.
My tears fall unchecked and unknown by you.
I haven't the strength to see my soul through.
I'll give you up now
I'll surrender I swear
And mourn your absence
For many a year.

Flashes

Have you ever been deeply in love?
As pure and white as a winged dove
Felt the grace of a bonsai tree
Like the touch of your hand that transforms me

Have you ever felt loves control?
Like a hymn that warms the soul
Like your eyes as they wash over me
Like butterflies when they're set free

Have you ever tasted bliss
In your lover's trembling kiss?
Felt the shiver
Legs a quiver
From an afternoon tryst

Will I ever be able to let go
Of all the things I've come to know
The sun dancing between us two
Shining dreams you made come true

Perhaps in time I will forget
My hair will grey my eyes will dim
My skin in wrinkles
My memories trim
But my heart will stay true until the end
My friend my lover, my lover my friend

Earthbound

Love
Pronounce the word carefully
With reverence and fear
The word that brought me to my knees
exposed my once happy life
And ripped it apart at the seams
Revealed i was but living in dreams
And with each new breath I take
Now that I am awake
I only know
You have changed me into a soul without a home
This deep void that is the absence of you
Once you revoked what you once invoked
This ill-timed lie that has become my truth
And how could I explain
In terms made plain
That because you are near
I am but a ghost?

Fallen

You called and I slinked into the kitchen
So no prying ears would have chance to listen
You whispered words of flattery and made your
demand
I made my excuses and left my man
My head empty but for thoughts of you
Never caring if my lies, he could see through
You made love to me and invoked a dark spirit I never
knew existed
The straight line I once walked now narrow and
twisted
I could feel the restraints all slipping away
Family, friends, God - none mattered today
Deeper and deeper down the rabbit hole I fall
Until only you exist and I am nothing at all

And I am not afraid of when I must wake
I am unafraid of the toll you will take
I hold no fear of the missed calls on my phone
My only fear, when you leave me alone.

I'll burn for you and you'll build the pyre
I'll taste the flames and drink the fire
I'll extinguish my past with barely a thought
And won't think twice about getting caught.

What more exists but this feeling we share?
Your hands on my skin, your fingers in my hair
No one else matters
Was I alive before?
Who draws the line
Between wife and whore?

Others tell me one day I will have much to regret
I'll open my eyes and start to suspect
All the perfection in you, my phenomenal lover
Was only uncommon skill under the cover.
I'll look back and note damage a hundred years could
not correct
And yet I cannot turn from this path I set.

Repetition

Imagining a life with you that will never be mine
A land in the future, a past span of time
Your chin on my head, your arm around my waist
My eyes tightly closed, my salty tears lay waste.

And you know what's so crazy, what's really insane?
That I don't want to stop
Too much to lose, too little to gain.

There is no resolution
Only rapturous pain
That I inflict
Time and time again.

Wilderness

I loved you with the heat of a million suns
And you burned them out slowly one by one
You could not see the Forrest from the trees
And wrapped my soul in iron chains
And brought me to my knees
And like the leaves that hide from the frost
I am the lone lioness - hungry, weak and lost
I am haunted and hunted by dreams past
And though this burden I long to shed - instead like a
shadow I cannot cast
I plod on slowly, unsteadily and unsure
This cold and long winter I cannot but endure

The Proposal

Revlon is not the only facet of my makeup
Just one aspect
I am a diamond uncut
In the rough
Have a seat
Lemme remove the imagery
Of the softer sex
Warping your mind
It would please me
If you believe me
When I say my worth is wrapped up in much more
than the silk between my thighs
Look north
What's behind my eyes?
The soul that beats, the strength that binds
Sweets take a seat
Get off your feet
Appreciate that I have the floor
We're both winners
Relax you don't have to keep score
Allow me to educate your mind
Saturate your thoughts with this precious find
I know it's been a long week
And we've both been on the grind
But taking me for granted
Is a game of dangerous design

I won't waste your time
Fighting about semantics
You want to call me a dime
It's all in how you define this
Sweetheart, lover, queen, boo
Babycakes, candy man
See I got names for you too
I want ya on the same page
Sharing the same dream
Giving each other what we crave
Let's not forget
It's us against the world
And when your back is to the wall
Tell me, who's your girl?
I'm not asking for anything I can't give
Let's live!
Put down your armor
Lower your shield
I'm not your enemy
Come to me
Let's lose ourselves in the dark
Ignite the spark
And in the light of day
We'll find a way
To try once more
Let's put the we before me and love one another even
more

Escape

Don't hide behind sensible words
Unlock your tongue
Caress the words as they escape
Allow me to inhale their magnificence
As they float toward me
Like clouds of sunshine
Warming my face
And stealing my breath
All at once the world dims
And I can live in this moment
With only you

Voyager

In this vast roiling variable sea
One must maneuver most decisively
With great care and little haste
Hoist a man to the mast
Allow him vision of all things future and past

The selkies melody seeks to entrap thee with sweet
promises of fleshy warmth
Close off to the siren's song
For only cold death perches upon thy boulders
Give her no purchase or quarter
Lay weight to port and stern

Seek thine compass within
Navigate the waves rise and fall
To a fairer day and a calm of sea
Oh my love, return to me

She

She is wrath unleashed, powerful, stealth and strong
to no man does she belong
a bloody tear trickles from her eye
not from sorrow, mind
born of anger which she will pay in kind
She was forged from fire and steel and stone
Cold and unfeeling and eternally alone
Conjured by the Gods to rectify the wrong
Death to the enslaver be her siren song
And perchance you cross her path
I beg you to make haste
For she suffers no fools
And may quickly lay you to waste
But do not be afraid, if just you be
For she is me and me is she.

About The Author

Amanda Sohan was born in the heart of New York City to a set of parents from British Guyana. While growing up with one foot steeped in the strict cultural boundaries her parents held dear and the other rooted in modern teenage American angst, reading and writing became the main medium for her journey toward freedom. In her dark poetry she grew to love the meaningful depths hidden in a collaboration of words. There was nothing more odd than the music she and her only sister Rowena grew up with. Two American, West Indian girls bumping to the sound of Eazy-E as Video Music Box flashed across the tube. Her teenage years, a graphic rebellion of words that could sneak under the radar of her parent's watchful eye. How ironic that her first work would be a gentle, humorous children's book. But stay turned as she intends to showcase her more adult side in her second book entitled HIM. The next pages are an excerpt from her soon to be released adult fiction book called "Him."

Excerpt from "Him"

Chapter 39 – It's Complicated

I "met" him on Facebook. I wanted to call that guy I met at Bogart's a million times but I wasn't entirely comfortable with that scenario just yet. Facebook seemed less risque, anonymous. I just needed to get back that pep in my step. I wanted to feel *wanted*. I needed a guy to make me feel sexy and alive again. It had been too long and I was starting to lose it. I smiled too hard at anyone with balls, stared two seconds too long and worse was the air of desperation that surrounded me like stale cigarettes. I needed to get back my mojo. Where is Taye Diggs??? Stella needs to get her groove back!

Anyhoo as per usual, I digress. So I met this dude on Facebook. He seemed harmless. He lived in Canada. I was in New York, safe distance away. He was attractive enough but not my style. He didn't give me the shivers but he did have fingers and could type fast. My requirements were at an all-time low.

At first our chats were quite innocent. I had my Facebook on my screen during work hours and when we had downtime we were able to chat. Coincidentally his name was Vijai. Good grief! You'd have thought the name alone would convey some inkling of dissatisfaction. It had not. Not long into the game he started asking me questions of a more personal nature. Normally I spurned such attentions. This time I welcomed them and found myself being quite candid about my situation. Who could have guessed that this would turn him on? His attention toward me intensified. We began texting each other consistently in the days ahead. After a couple of days he asked if I would grant him permission to call me. I hesitated for a few minutes before granting his request. I wasn't sure what I wanted but I figured this must be the next logical step right? Who wanted to text forever? I asked him to call me around 10 when I had already closed the kitchen, kissed the kid goodnight and the rest of the evening belonged to me. He agreed.

I took a quick shower, got into my shorts and tank and hopped into bed with five minutes to spare. My phone buzzed at exactly 10pm.

I dropped my voice an octave in what I hoped sounded at least interesting if not appealing.

"Hey Vijai." I answered. He was prompt.

"Hi Amanda. It's nice to hear your voice after communicating with you for so long in text and chat."

My first impression of his voice was that it sounded a bit bland. I was neither impressed nor disappointed, which in and of itself was disappointing. I hadn't realized I was hoping it would have some appeal. *I must dissect and analyze later.*

Secondly I thought to myself we've only been chatting for a week, what do you mean by *so long*? I silently chided myself. *Really bitch?* How many boxes have to be ticked in order to converse? I hushed my inner Sasha Fierce and played along.

"Nice to hear your voice too. So what are you up to tonight?"

"Amanda?"

"Yes."

"Where are your hands?"

"What? Why?" Okay now this was getting weird. I started looking at my free hand like it was going to do something independent of my command.

"Pull down your panties and touch yourself for me? Don't you want me to make you feel good?"

What the fuck?

"Umm, what?"

His tone became even more assertive.

"Pull down your panties for me babe. Touch yourself. Are you wet? Did I make you wet?"

Was this fool for real? I couldn't contain my laughter any longer.

"What? You're not turned on?" He asked, adopting a more appropriate and humble tone.

"Dude, no. I just started talking to you and you're gonna come at me like that?"

"I know, I know. But I figured you've been through a lot and by yourself for a while. I was hoping you would think it was fun."

"Well honestly I've never really done the whole phone sex thing but if I'm gonna go that route with anyone I'd definitely have to be comfortable with them. You can't just hit me with all of that during our first conversation."

"Yeah I guess. Sorry."

I laughed. He wasn't a jerk but I didn't quite know how to feel about what just transpired. What was clear is that I'd had enough for one evening. Justified was coming up and this wasn't worth missing one second of Timothy Olyphant.

"It's alright dude. No harm, no foul. I'm gonna say goodnight now. We'll chat another time."

"Oh ok, hope so. Goodnight." He replied, disappointed.

"Goodnight." I said as kindly as I could before hanging up. He wasn't important enough where his feelings would matter above my own but I didn't want to be a dick about it.

I checked C's Facebook before shutting off my phone. My eyes widened. On his Timeline it didn't even have his status as a married man anymore. He hadn't changed it to *Single* or *It's Complicated*, he avoided the quandary by just omitting his status entirely.

Awesome sauce! *NOT!* I checked the time on my phone. Still had 15 minutes before Justified. I flung the covers off, jumped out of bed and wiggled out of my poom-poom shorts. I rummaged through my bottom drawer before grabbing my prize and leaping back into bed. I took a second to engage the lock on my door and another minute to search for a appealing porn video. I was wound far too tight. I needed a release and I sure as shit wasn't gonna get it from that lame ass conversation with Vijai. Exit stage left. I've got business I must attend to. I'll be damned if this night was going to be a complete bust.